BASKETBALL

Alison Hawes

Editorial consultants: Cliff Moon,
Lorraine Petersen and Frances Ridley

RISING ★ STARS

nasen

NASEN House, 4/5 Amber Business Village, Amber Close, Amington, Tamworth, Staffordshire B77 4RP

Rising Stars UK Ltd.
22 Grafton Street, London W1S 4EX
www.risingstars-uk.com

Every effort has been made to trace copyright holders and obtain their permission for use of copyright material. The publisher will gladly receive information enabling them to rectify any error or omission in subsequent editions.
All facts are correct at time of going to press.

Published 2007

Cover design: Button plc
Cover image: Alamy
Text design and typesetting: Andy Wilson
Publisher: Gill Budgell
Project management and editorial: Lesley Densham
Editing: Clare Robertson
Editorial consultants: Cliff Moon, Lorraine Petersen and Frances Ridley
Technical adviser: With many thanks to Alan Sweetman-Hicks, Assistant Coach with Worthing Thunder Basketball Team
Illustrations: Patrick Boyer: pages 24–25, 32–33, 38–41
Oxford Illustrators and Designers: pages 8, 12
Photos: Alamy: pages 4–5, 9, 10, 11, 13, 20, 29,
Corbis: pages 4, 5, 12, 14, 15, 35, 42, 43
Empics: pages 6, 18, 19, 21, 22, 23, 26–27, 34, 36, 37
Getty Images: pages 8, 9, 11, 16, 17, 18, 19, 30, 31
Andre Nichols: page 28

This book should not be used as a guide to the sports shown in it.
The publisher accepts no responsibility for any harm which might result from taking part in these sports.

British Library Cataloguing in Publication Data.
A CIP record for this book is available from the British Library.

ISBN: 978-1-84680-192-1

Printed by Craft Print International Limited, Singapore

Contents

Basketball

Basketball is a team sport.

It is fast and action-packed.

Basketball facts!

Basketball is an American sport.

It was invented in 1891 by a PE teacher called James Naismith.

He used a football and peach baskets!

Basketball is for everyone.

It is played by men, women, girls and boys.

If you want to play for a team you will need to be fit, and practise those moves!

Basketball kit

You don't need a lot of kit
to play basketball.

A light, loose vest keeps you
cool and lets you move easily.

Light, loose shorts keep you
cool and let you move easily.

Soft, thick socks stop
your feet getting blisters.

Air-cushioned trainers
stop your feet getting sore.

Play safe!

✗ No zips
✗ No buttons
✗ No watches
✗ No jewellery
✗ No loose laces

Basketball court

Basketball is played on a court.

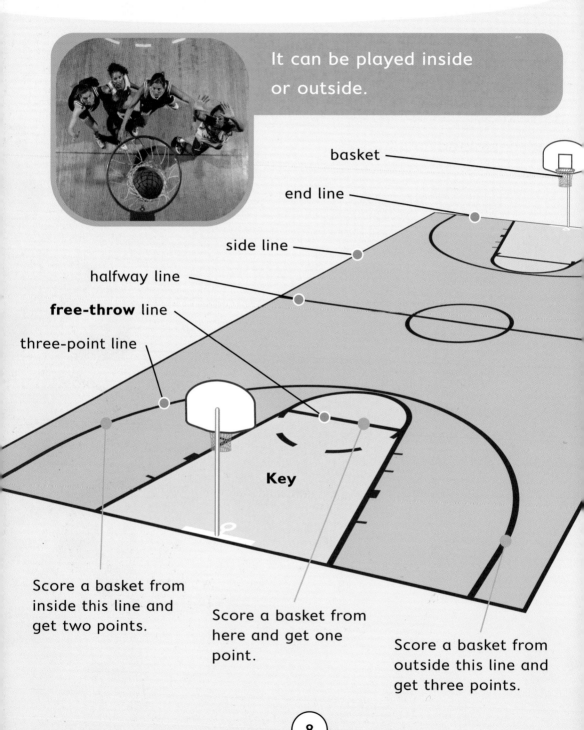

It can be played inside or outside.

basket

end line

side line

halfway line

free-throw line

three-point line

Key

Score a basket from inside this line and get two points.

Score a basket from here and get one point.

Score a basket from outside this line and get three points.

The basket

The basket is made up of a hoop and a net.

The hoop is 3.05 metres from the ground.

The basket has a backboard which is made of wood or plastic.

backboard

hoop

net

The ball

A basketball is made from rubber or leather.

It is full of air. But it still weighs up to 650 grams! (That's as heavy as a pair of your shoes.)

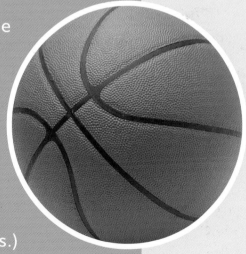

Basketball clubs

School

Some schools run a basketball club. This is a good place to learn all the basic moves.

You can play against teams from other schools.

Sports centre

Some sports centres run a basketball club after school. This is another good place to learn the moves and play for a team.

Look on the Internet to find your local club.

No club?

In the park

A park is a good place to practise the basic moves.

Some parks have a basketball court. Others just have a hoop and backboard.

At home

Get some mates round and practise those shots!

The team

A basketball team has up to 12 players.

Just five players are on court at a time.
They play in different positions on the court.

Team positions

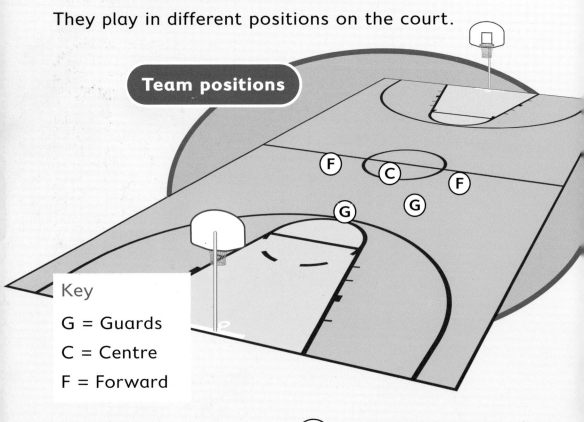

Key

G = Guards
C = Centre
F = Forward

The guards tend to be smaller, quicker players.

They are good at dribbling and passing.

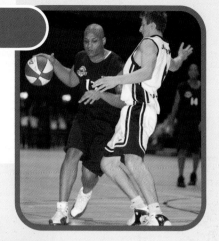

Forward

The forwards tend to be taller players.

They are good at shooting, passing and getting the **rebounds**.

Centre

The centres tend to be the tallest players.

They are good at jumping, shooting and getting the rebounds.

But a basketball team plays all over the court. Everyone needs to be good at all the basic moves.

The moves

Passing

In a fast game like basketball, you must keep the ball moving.

So get passing!

The chest pass

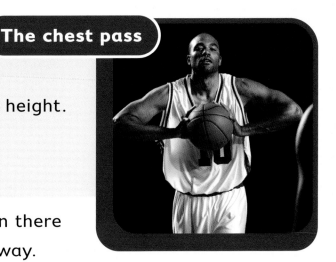

Use two hands.

Hold the ball at chest height.

Push the ball to your team-mate.

Use a chest pass when there is no defender in the way.

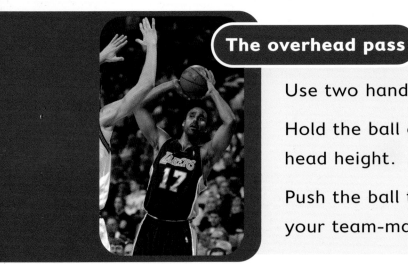

The overhead pass

Use two hands.

Hold the ball at head height.

Push the ball to your team-mate.

Use an overhead pass when there is a defender close to you.

Use one or two hands.

Hold the ball at
hip height.

Bounce the ball to
your team-mate.

Use a bounce pass when you need to get
round a defender or under a defender's arms.

Dribbling

Use one hand to
bounce the ball.

Keep the ball close
to you as you run.

Only dribble when you
can't pass!

Passing is quicker
than dribbling.

Shooting

Basketball is won by scoring points.

You score points by getting the ball into the basket.

So get shooting!

The lay-up shot

Use this shot when there is no defender in your way.

The set shot

Use this shot for a free throw if you are close to the net.

The jump shot

Use this shot if there is a defender very close to you.

Defending

When the other team has the ball,
you must stop them scoring.

So get defending!

When to defend	How to defend
When the other player is shooting	◎ Use your arms and jump to stop the ball
When the other player is passing	◎ Bend or jump to stop the ball ◎ Use your arms
When the other player is dribbling	◎ Bend down and get in close ◎ Use your arms
When the other player misses a shot	◎ Keep your eyes open ◎ Get ready to catch the ball when it rebounds

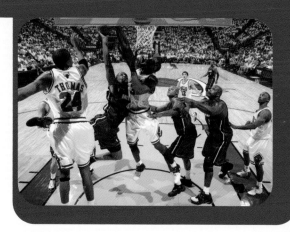

Flash moves

All the top players are good at the basic moves. But they are good at flash moves like these too.

Slam dunk

A slam dunk is a flash shot.

Players jump above the basket and stuff the ball in the net.

Reverse jam

The reverse jam is an even flashier shot.

Players do a slam dunk with their back to the basket.

Hook shot

A lot of the top players use this shot to score a basket when a defender is very close to them.

Flash dribbling

Some players can dribble the ball behind their back or between their legs!

Basketball fact!

In 2003, an American basketball player dribbled a basketball 174 kilometres in 24 hours!

Against the clock!

Basketball is fast because it is played against the clock.

So move fast! Think fast!

If you run out of time, the ball goes to the other team.

8 The eight-second rule

When your team has the ball, they have just eight seconds to get it over the halfway line.

The 24-second rule

When your team has the ball, they have just 24 seconds to shoot at the basket.

24

The five-second rule

When you get the ball, you have just five seconds to start to pass, shoot or dribble it.

The three-second rule

When your team has the ball, no one on your team can be in the other team's **key** for more than three seconds.

Time-out

Your team can call **time-out** five times in a match.

Each time-out lasts one minute.

Teams use a time-out to talk **tactics**!

Wheelchair basketball

Wheelchair basketball is a fast, action-packed sport.

Many players use a special sports wheelchair.

A sports wheelchair is light and easy to move around in.

Basketball fact!

Wheelchair basketball was invented to help soldiers wounded in World War II to get better.

Basketball fact!

The Great Britain men's wheelchair basketball team won a medal at the 2004 **Paralympics**.

Wheelchair basketball is now played in over 80 countries.

Ade Adepitan helped Great Britain win bronze in the 2004 Paralympics.

A Bad Move (Part one)

Josh's dad had a new job. It was miles from their house, so they had to move.

Josh's mum and dad wanted to move.
Even Josh's kid sister, Liz, wanted to move.

But Josh didn't. He hated the idea.

Josh said, "If we move, I'll miss my mates.
And I won't get to play basketball for
the Tigers again!"

But like it or not, Josh had to move.

At the new house, Dad put up Josh's old basketball hoop.

"There you are," said Dad. "That should make you feel a bit more at home!"

But Josh just walked away.

He knew his dad was trying to help.
But it was no good.

He just didn't want to be there.

Continued on page 32

Going to a game

Going to a top basketball game
is fun – and noisy!

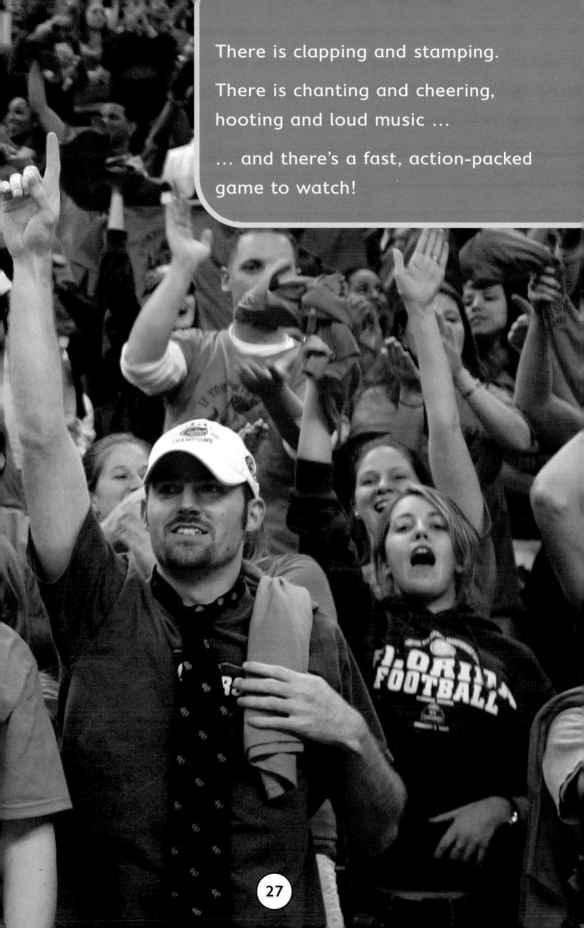

There is clapping and stamping.

There is chanting and cheering, hooting and loud music ...

... and there's a fast, action-packed game to watch!

Basketball people

Lots of people help out at a basketball game.

Timekeepers

There are two timekeepers on the court.

One stops and starts the game clock and times the **time-outs**.

The other stops and starts the 24-second clock.

Scorer

The scorer counts the score, the fouls and the time-outs.

The coach trains the team and decides on team **tactics**.

The coach decides when the **subs** go on and when time-out is called.

Referees

The referees control the game.

They make sure the players stick to the rules.

Referees' signals

The referees use a whistle and hand signals to control the game.

See if you can spot any of these signals if you watch a match.

Some common hand signals

one free throw

two free throws

time-out

Hand signals
for fouls

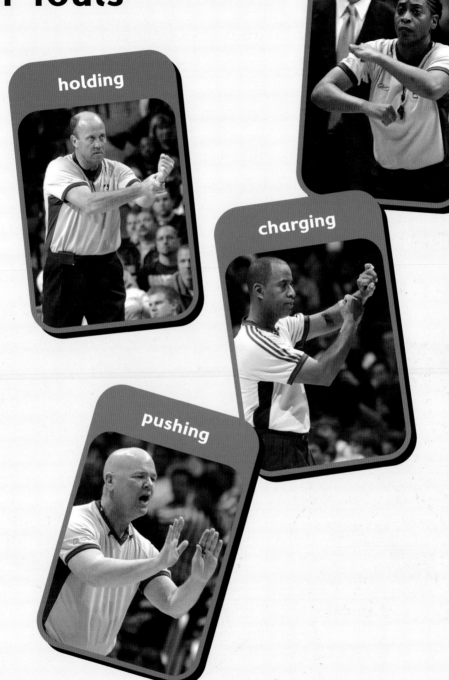

travelling

holding

charging

pushing

A Bad Move (Part two)

The next day, Josh was in a better mood.

He went into the garden to practise his basketball shots.

He remembered what the Tiger's coach had told him and took a shot.

There was a clonk.

The ball hit the backboard and dropped into the net.

The boy next door heard the clonk and looked over the fence.

He watched, as five shots out of five dropped into the net!

"You're good," he called. "But not as good as Michael Jordan. He could net a shot with his eyes shut!"

Josh grinned and shut his eyes.

There was a clonk as the ball hit a window.

Josh opened his eyes.

There was a crack in the window!

Josh grabbed his basketball.

"Quick, let's get out of here!" he said.

Continued on page 38

Michael Jordan

Michael Jordan is an American basketball player.

He is the most famous basketball player in the world.

People say Jordan can shoot baskets with his eyes shut!

Basketball facts!

Michael Jordan wears size 13 trainers.

Air Jordan trainers are named after him.

Michael Jordan fact file

Born	**17 February 1963, New York**
Height	**1.98 metres**
Weight	**98.18 kilos**
Basketball position	**Shooting guard**
Average points scored in a match	**30.1**
Teams he played for	**University of North Carolina Chicago Bulls Washington Wizards**
Retired	**2003**

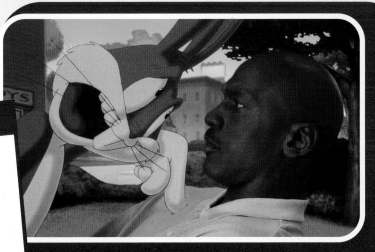

Did you know?

Michael was in a film with Bugs Bunny.

The film was called 'Space Jam'.

Harlem Globetrotters

The Harlem Globetrotters are an American basketball team.

They're the most famous basketball team in the world.

The Globetrotters are famous for their basketball shows.

The shows are full of flash moves, trick shots and stunts.

The Harlem Globetrotters have helped make basketball popular outside America.

They began playing basketball around the world in the 1950s and a team still tours the world today.

Basketball facts!

A Harlem Globetrotter holds the world record for a 3.65 metre vertical slam dunk.

The tallest player to play for the Harlem Globetrotters was Dut Mayer. He is 2.29 metres tall!

A Bad Move
(Part three)

The two boys ran down the road.

"I'm Max," said the boy from next door.
"We'll go to the park – Zac is playing there."

Josh and Max watched Zac and his mates.
They were all good players.

Josh asked if he and Max could join in.

Zac looked at Josh and Max and laughed.

"Sorry, mate. You two are too small to play basketball."

"But that's rubbish!" said Josh. "You don't have to be a giant to play basketball!"

But it was no good.

Zac just walked away.

"Come back when you've grown a bit!" he laughed.

Continued on the next page

Later that week, Josh and Max went to the fair.

Josh's dad said they had to take Liz too. He was still angry about the broken window.

Zac and his mates were there.

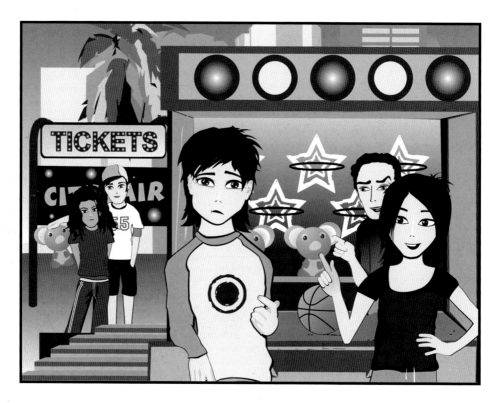

Liz saw Zac win a prize at the basketball game.

"Win me a prize!" Liz said to Josh.

"Yes! Win your girlfriend a prize!" laughed Zac.

Josh felt like hitting him.

Josh breathed deeply and took a shot.

There was a clonk as the ball hit
the backboard and dropped into the net.

Josh shot five baskets out of five.

Zac and his mates had stopped laughing.

Zac went up to Josh.

"I was wrong about you, mate," he said.

"We play for a team
at the sports
centre. Why don't
you come along
next week?"

"I'll think about it,"
Josh said.

Josh, Max and Liz
walked away.

"I think I'm going
to like it here!"
Josh grinned.

Olympic Games

Basketball became an Olympic sport for men in 1936.

The American team won the first gold medal for basketball.

The man who invented basketball was at the 1936 Olympic Games.

He gave the American team their gold medals.

Basketball facts!

At the 1936 Olympics, players taller than 1.87 metres were not allowed to play.

At the 1936 Olympics, basketball was played outside on sand!

The Americans played their best team ever in the 1992 Olympics.

This team was so good it was called the Dream Team!

They easily won all their eight games and the gold medal.

Michael Jordan was in the Dream Team.

Quiz

1 What kind of sport is basketball?

2 Who invented basketball?

3 How high from the ground is a basketball hoop?

4 What do forwards need to be good at?

5 Which is quicker, passing or dribbling?

6 What is a slam dunk?

7 Why does a coach call time-out?

8 Why was wheelchair basketball first invented?

9 What is the referees' signal for pushing?

10 What size trainers does Michael Jordan wear?

Glossary of terms

free throw   A free shot at a basket. A free throw can be given by the referee when he/she sees a foul. Free throws are taken from the free-throw line on the court.

key   The restricted area on a basketball court. (See the shaded area on the diagram of a court on page 8.)

Paralympics   The Olympics for people with disabilities.

rebound   A ball that hits the rim of the basket or the backboard and bounces back into the court when a shot at the basket is missed.

subs   This is short for 'substitutes'. The substitutes are the players that sit on the side lines until they are chosen to swap places with a player on court.

tactics   How teams plan to use their skills to beat their opponents.

time-out   When the game is stopped. Teams can take five time-outs in a match to discuss tactics. This is called 'charged time-out'. The referee can also call time-out when a player is injured.

More resources

Books

Basketball
Clive Gifford
Published by Hodder (Activators series) (ISBN: 978-0340736302)
Lots of black and white drawings. Good on basic moves.
Gives games to practise the basic skills.

Basketball
David Titmuss
Published by Cassell Illustrated ('Play the game' series)
(ISBN: 978-0706377170)
Lots of great colour photos. Good on basic moves.

Ultimate Basketball
Published by Dorling Kindersley (ISBN: 978-0789496522)
Full of photos. Good on the history of the game.

Magazines

Slam (Primedia, Inc.)
This is an American basketball magazine. It is full of NBA news,
interviews with NBA players and lots of great photos.

Websites

www.news.bbc.co.uk/sports1/hi/other_sports/basketball
This is the BBC Sports Academy Basketball website.
Excellent tips and info. Lots of animations of shots and moves.

www.NBA.com
If you are into American basketball this is the site for photos and
news of all the American NBA stars.

www.FIBA.com
International basketball website. News and interviews.
Good on the rules.

www.englandbasketball.co.uk
News, results and league tables. Good section on history of the game.

DVDs

Space Jam (Cert U)
Warner (Cat. no. B00004CXMW)
A fun family movie, mixing cartoon characters and real-life top basketball
players like Michael Jordan.

Coach Carter (Cert 12)
Paramount (Cat. no. B0009IGXKY)
This movie is based on the true story of Ken Carter, a basketball coach to
a struggling school team. Good story and plenty of basketball action.

Answers

1 A team game

2 James Naismith

3 3.05 metres

4 They need to be good at shooting, passing and getting the rebounds.

5 Passing is quicker than dribbling.

6 When the player scores a basket by jumping above the basket and stuffing the ball down into the net

7 To talk team tactics or because a player is injured

8 To help injured World War II soldiers get better

9 Both arms out in front; hands facing forwards in a pushing motion

10 Size 13

Index